MITCHELL C.
HENDERSON

THE FINANCIAL

$

FREEDOM

PLAYBOOK

A GUIDE TO SMART
INVESTING FOR **BEGINNERS**

The Financial Freedom Playbook: A Guide to Smart Investing for Beginners

Copyright © 2024

All rights reserved.

No part of this book may be reproduced in any form without permission, except brief quotations for review purposes.

ISBN: 9798304894142

Disclaimer:

This book is for educational and motivational purposes only. It does not constitute financial advice. Readers should consult a qualified financial advisor before making financial decisions.

This book is dedicated to all who wish to take control of their future

Contents

Introduction
    Why Investing is the Key to Financial Freedom   *7*

Chapter 1
    Understanding the Basics of Investing   *9*

Chapter 2
    Getting Your Financial House in Order Before Investing   *13*

Chapter 3
    Starting Small: How to Invest With Minimal Resources   *18*

Chapter 4
    Stock Market 101   *23*

Chapter 5
    Real Estate Investing Made Simple   *30*

Chapter 6
    Other Passive Income Streams to Explore   *37*

Chapter 7
    Navigating Risk and Building Confidence as an Investor   *43*

Chapter 8
    Building Your Investment Portfolio   *49*

Chapter 9
    Tax Basics Every Investor Should Know   *55*

Chapter 10
    Staying the Course and Growing Your Wealth   *62*

Chapter 11
    A Step-by-Step Guide to Your First Investment   *68*

Conclusion
    Investing is for Everyone   *75*

Bonus Material
    Investment Checklist   *79*

Introduction

Why Investing is the Key to Financial Freedom

When it comes to building a secure and prosperous future, investing is not just an option—it's a necessity. Imagine your money working tirelessly for you, growing while you sleep, and paving the way for financial independence. This is the power of investing. Unlike saving, which simply stores money for future use, investing multiplies your resources, enabling you to achieve goals that might otherwise seem out of reach.

In today's economy, saving alone is no longer enough. Inflation steadily erodes the value of idle money, and the cost of living continues to rise. While saving is essential for short-term security, such as building an emergency fund, it won't get you to your dream retirement or fund the life you envision. To break free from financial limitations and take control of your future, investing is the bridge you must cross.

But for many, the word "investing" feels intimidating. You might have heard, *"It's too risky,"* or *"I need to be rich to start."* These myths have kept countless people stuck in financial stagnation. The truth? Investing is for everyone—regardless of your current income, education, or background. Starting small and staying consistent can lead to life-changing results over time. The earlier you start, the more you stand to gain.

This book is your personal guide to navigating the world of investing. You don't need a degree in finance or a fortune to get started. What you need is a clear roadmap, practical advice, and the confidence to take the first step. That's exactly what this book will provide. Together, we'll break down complex concepts into simple, actionable steps. You'll learn how to build wealth with minimal resources, understand the risks and rewards, and develop strategies tailored to your unique goals.

Whether you're just beginning your financial journey or looking to take your first steps into the world of investing, this book will empower you to act. By the end of our time together, you'll not only understand how to make your money work for you but also gain the confidence to make smart investment decisions.

Let's dispel the myths, conquer the fear, and chart a course toward financial freedom. The path to building wealth starts here. Are you ready? Let's dive in.

Chapter 1
Understanding the Basics of Investing

If you've ever dreamed of living a life free from financial worry, investing is the key to making that dream a reality. But let's start with the basics: **what is investing?** At its core, investing is putting your money to work to generate more money. It's the process of using your resources—whether big or small—to create opportunities for growth. Investing allows you to plant seeds today that will grow into a financial harvest tomorrow.

Saving is like storing your money in a jar. It's safe, but it doesn't grow. Investing, on the other hand, is like planting a tree. Over time, it grows, produces fruit, and even creates shade for the future. When done wisely, investing transforms money from a static resource into a dynamic tool, compounding and multiplying over the years.

The Power of Compound Interest: Make Your Money Work for You

Albert Einstein famously called compound interest "the eighth wonder of the world." Why? Because it has the power to turn modest investments into life-changing sums.

Here's how it works: imagine you invest $100, and it earns 10% interest in a year. At the end of the year, you have $110. If you leave that $110 invested, the next year, you'll earn interest not just on your original $100, but also on the $10 you earned previously. Over time, this compounding effect accelerates, growing your wealth exponentially.

The earlier you start investing, the more powerful compound interest becomes. Even small contributions can grow into significant amounts if given enough time. This is why waiting to invest is one of the most expensive decisions you can make. Remember: time is your greatest ally in the world of investing.

Risk vs. Reward: Understanding the Trade-Offs

Every investment comes with a balance of risk and reward. The higher the potential return, the greater the risk you're likely to face. This is why understanding your risk tolerance is so important. Are you comfortable with short-term ups and downs in exchange for potentially higher long-term gains? Or do you prefer the safety of steady, predictable growth, even if it means smaller returns?

The good news is that risk doesn't have to be scary—it can be managed. Diversifying your investments, starting with smaller amounts, and focusing on long-term goals are all ways to reduce risk. Think of it like crossing a river. You can't avoid the current entirely, but with the right tools and strategies, you can get to the other side safely.

Key Terms Made Simple

The world of investing can feel like it's full of complicated jargon, but it doesn't have to be. Let's break down a few essential terms:

- **Assets**: Things you own that can grow in value over time, like stocks, real estate, or a business.
- **Liabilities**: Things you owe, like debt or expenses, that take money out of your pocket.
- **ROI (Return on Investment)**: A way to measure how much money you make compared to what you invested. For example, if you invest $100 and earn $10, your ROI is 10%.

- **Diversification**: Spreading your money across different types of investments to reduce risk. Think of it as not putting all your eggs in one basket.
- **Compound Interest**: As mentioned earlier, this is the magic of earning interest on both your initial investment and the interest it generates over time.

Understanding these terms is like learning the rules of a game. Once you know how to play, you'll feel empowered to make smarter decisions and start winning.

Investing isn't reserved for the rich or the experts—it's a tool anyone can use to achieve their goals. With a basic understanding of how investing works, you've already taken your first step toward financial freedom. In the next chapter, we'll lay the foundation you need to start investing confidently, including clearing debt, setting goals, and creating a budget that frees up money for your investments.

Your future is waiting. Let's build it together.

Chapter 2

Getting Your Financial House in Order Before Investing

Investing is an exciting journey, but before you set off, it's essential to lay a solid foundation. Think of this step as building a sturdy base for a skyscraper—you can't reach great heights without it. Getting your financial house in order ensures that your investments are not just successful but sustainable, setting you up for long-term financial freedom.

The Foundation: Building an Emergency Fund and Clearing High-Interest Debt

Before you put your money into the stock market, real estate, or any other investment, you need to protect yourself from life's inevitable surprises. A sudden car repair, medical expense, or job loss can derail your financial progress if you're not prepared. That's why your first priority should be building an emergency fund

—three to six months' worth of essential living expenses set aside in a safe, easily accessible account.

Next, tackle high-interest debt, like credit cards or payday loans. These debts can erode your financial progress faster than any investment can grow your wealth. If your credit card charges 20% interest, paying it off is like getting a guaranteed 20% return on your money—something no investment can reliably match.

Clearing debt and building an emergency fund may feel like slow progress at first, but it's one of the most powerful steps you can take. These actions free you from financial stress and create the space you need to invest confidently and effectively.

How to Calculate Your Risk Tolerance: Knowing What Kind of Investor You Are

Not all investors are created equal, and that's okay. Some people thrive on the thrill of high-risk, high-reward opportunities, while others prefer the steady growth of safer investments. Understanding your risk tolerance is essential for making decisions that align with your personality and financial goals.

Ask yourself these questions:

- How would I feel if my investment lost 10%, 20%, or even 50% of its value in the short term?

- How soon will I need access to the money I'm investing?
- Am I willing to take on more risk for the potential of higher returns, or would I prefer smaller, more predictable gains?

If you're unsure, many online tools and apps can help you assess your risk tolerance. Remember, there's no "right" answer—it's about finding what works for you. And as you gain experience and confidence, your tolerance for risk may evolve.

Setting Financial Goals: Short-Term, Mid-Term, and Long-Term

Investing without a clear goal is like setting sail without a destination. Before you start, take the time to define your *why*. What are you investing for?

- **Short-Term Goals**: These might include saving for a vacation, a wedding, or building your emergency fund. For these goals, safer investments like high-yield savings accounts or treasury bills are ideal.
- **Mid-Term Goals**: Buying a home, starting a business, or funding a child's education are examples of mid-term goals. These require investments with moderate risk and growth potential, like index funds or bonds.

- **Long-Term Goals**: Retirement, financial independence, or creating generational wealth fall into this category. Long-term goals benefit most from the power of compound interest and the growth potential of higher-risk investments like stocks or real estate.

Once your goals are clear, you can match your investments to your timeline and risk tolerance. This alignment ensures every dollar you invest is working toward something meaningful.

Creating a Simple Budget to Free Up Money for Investing

One of the biggest myths about investing is that you need a lot of money to start. The truth is, small, consistent contributions can lead to significant results over time. The key is finding that extra cash to invest—and that's where budgeting comes in.

Start by tracking your income and expenses. Identify areas where you can cut back without sacrificing your quality of life. Could you skip the daily coffee shop visit and brew at home? Cancel unused subscriptions? Cook more meals instead of eating out?

Create a simple budget with these categories:

1. **Essentials**: Rent/mortgage, utilities, groceries, transportation.
2. **Debt Repayment**: Focus on clearing high-interest debt.
3. **Savings**: Build your emergency fund.
4. **Investments**: Allocate even a small amount to start growing your wealth.

Automating your finances can make this process even easier. Set up automatic transfers to your investment account so that saving and investing become effortless habits.

By getting your financial house in order, you're creating a launchpad for success. You'll have the confidence of knowing you're prepared for life's challenges and the freedom to invest without fear. In the next chapter, we'll explore how to start investing with minimal resources—because you don't need to be rich to begin building wealth.

Your foundation is set. Now, let's build on it!

Chapter 3

Starting Small: How to Invest with Minimal Resources

One of the biggest misconceptions about investing is that you need to be wealthy to begin. This myth has kept far too many people on the sidelines, waiting for the "right time" when they have more money. Here's the truth: you don't need a fortune to start investing. In fact, some of the world's most successful investors began with just a few dollars and a commitment to consistency.

Investing is not about how much you start with; it's about starting—period. The magic of compound interest, consistency, and time are far more powerful than the size of your initial investment. Today, you have access to tools and strategies that make it easier than ever to grow wealth, even with minimal resources.

Debunking the Myth That You Need a Lot of Money to Start

Let's put this myth to rest. Investing isn't reserved for the elite—it's accessible to everyone. Thanks to technology and innovation, the barriers to entry have never been lower.

In the past, investing often required significant sums of money, high fees, and exclusive access to financial advisors. But today, you can start with as little as $5. That's less than the cost of a cup of coffee! Micro-investing platforms, fractional shares, and fee-free brokerages have leveled the playing field, making it possible for anyone to build wealth, no matter their starting point.

The key to success isn't having a large sum to invest upfront; it's about developing the habit of investing regularly. Small amounts, invested consistently, can grow into life-changing wealth over time.

Micro-Investing Platforms: Apps and Tools for Investing Small Amounts

Thanks to the rise of micro-investing, you don't need to be a financial guru to start. These platforms allow you to invest small amounts of money in stocks, ETFs, or even real estate with just a few taps on your phone. Here are some beginner-friendly options:

- **Acorns**: Automatically rounds up your everyday purchases and invests the spare change into diversified portfolios.
- **Stash**: Allows you to start with as little as $1 and offers educational tools to help you learn as you invest.
- **Robinhood**: A commission-free platform where you can buy fractional shares of your favorite companies.
- **Public**: Combines investing with a social media experience, letting you see what others are investing in.

These apps remove the intimidation factor and make investing accessible to everyone. They also eliminate high fees, allowing you to keep more of your hard-earned money.

Dollar-Cost Averaging: Why Consistency Beats Timing the Market

When it comes to investing, trying to predict the perfect moment to buy or sell is a losing game. Even seasoned investors struggle to time the market successfully. Instead of waiting for the "right time," focus on being consistent with your investments. This is where **dollar-cost averaging** comes in.

Dollar-cost averaging is a simple yet powerful strategy where you invest a fixed amount of money at regular intervals, regardless of market conditions. When prices are high, your fixed amount buys fewer shares. When prices are low, it buys more. Over time, this strategy averages out the cost of your investments, reducing the impact of market volatility.

For example, let's say you invest $50 every month in an index fund. Some months, the price per share might be higher, and other months it might be lower. But by staying consistent, you take advantage of the market's natural ups and downs, building wealth steadily over time.

The beauty of dollar-cost averaging is that it takes emotion out of investing. You don't have to worry about when to invest because you're doing it automatically and consistently.

Success Stories of People Who Started Small and Grew Big

The idea of starting small might seem too good to be true, but history is full of examples of ordinary people who built extraordinary wealth by investing consistently over time.

Take the story of **Grace Groner**, a secretary who lived modestly and invested small amounts in stocks throughout her life. When she passed away, her portfolio was worth over $7 million—all because she started early, stayed consistent, and let time work its magic.

Or consider **Ronald Read**, a janitor and gas station attendant who amassed an $8 million fortune by investing in dividend-paying stocks. He didn't earn a high salary, but he invested consistently and let compound interest do the rest.

These stories aren't anomalies—they're proof that anyone can achieve financial freedom by starting where they are and staying the course.

Starting small doesn't mean thinking small. Every great financial journey begins with a single step. By investing even modest amounts, leveraging today's accessible tools, and staying consistent through dollar-cost averaging, you're building a foundation for long-term wealth.

In the next chapter, we'll dive deeper into one of the most popular and powerful wealth-building tools: the stock market. You'll learn the basics of stocks, index funds, and how to start making informed decisions.

You've started small. Now, let's think big!

Chapter 4
Stock Market 101

For many, the stock market feels like an intimidating maze, full of jargon and unpredictable movements. But in reality, it's one of the most powerful tools for building wealth and achieving financial freedom. The good news? You don't need to be a Wall Street professional to understand it. By grasping the basics, you can start making informed decisions and harness the market's potential for long-term growth.

This chapter will break down the fundamentals of the stock market, demystify key concepts, and equip you with the tools to start investing with confidence.

What Are Stocks? Understanding Shares, Indices, and the Stock Exchange

At its core, a stock represents ownership in a company. When you buy a share of stock, you're essentially purchasing a small piece of that business. As the company grows and becomes more profitable, the value of your shares can increase, allowing you to benefit from their success.

The stock market is where these transactions take place. Think of it as a giant marketplace where companies sell shares to raise money, and investors buy and sell those shares based on their expectations of the company's future performance. Major stock exchanges like the **New York Stock Exchange (NYSE)** or **Nasdaq** facilitate these trades.

You'll often hear about stock indices, such as the **S&P 500** or the **Dow Jones Industrial Average**. These indices track the performance of a group of stocks, giving investors a snapshot of how a particular segment of the market is doing. For example:

- **The S&P 500** tracks the 500 largest publicly traded companies in the U.S.
- **The Dow Jones Industrial Average** monitors 30 major companies, often considered leaders in their industries.

Understanding these basics lays the groundwork for making smart investment choices.

Types of Stocks: Blue-Chip, Growth, Dividend-Paying Stocks, and More

Not all stocks are created equal. Each type has unique characteristics that appeal to different kinds of investors:

1. **Blue-Chip Stocks**: These are shares of well-established, financially stable companies with a history of consistent performance. Think of household names like Apple, Coca-Cola, and Johnson & Johnson. Blue-chip stocks are often less volatile and a good choice for long-term stability.

2. **Growth Stocks**: These represent companies expected to grow at a faster rate than the overall market. They often reinvest their profits into expansion rather than paying dividends. Growth stocks can offer high returns but also come with higher risk. Examples include technology startups or innovative firms in emerging industries.

3. **Dividend-Paying Stocks**: These stocks pay regular dividends, which are portions of a company's earnings distributed to shareholders. They're ideal for investors looking for steady income and are often found in sectors like utilities, healthcare, or consumer goods.

4. **Value Stocks**: These are stocks that investors believe are undervalued compared to their true

worth. Buying value stocks is like finding a diamond in the rough—they can offer significant returns if the market eventually recognizes their potential.

By diversifying across these types, you can balance risk and reward while tailoring your portfolio to your financial goals.

ETFs and Index Funds: The Beginner's Best Friend for Diversified Investing

If picking individual stocks feels overwhelming, you're not alone. That's where **ETFs (Exchange-Traded Funds)** and **index funds** come in. These investment vehicles are perfect for beginners because they offer instant diversification and require little ongoing management.

- **Index Funds**: These funds aim to replicate the performance of a specific market index, such as the S&P 500. When you invest in an index fund, you're essentially buying a small piece of every company in that index. This diversification reduces risk and provides exposure to the overall market's growth.

- **ETFs**: Similar to index funds, ETFs bundle multiple stocks or assets into one investment. The key difference is that ETFs trade on stock exchanges like individual stocks, making them more flexible.

Both options are cost-effective, beginner-friendly, and ideal for long-term investors. With index funds or ETFs, you don't have to worry about picking the next big stock—your portfolio grows in tandem with the broader market.

How to Research Stocks: Basic Tools and Strategies

While ETFs and index funds are great for diversification, many investors also enjoy picking individual stocks. To make informed decisions, it's important to do your homework. Here are some tools and strategies to get you started:

1. **Learn the Basics of Fundamental Analysis**
   - **Earnings**: Is the company consistently profitable?
   - **Revenue Growth**: Are sales increasing over time?
   - **Debt Levels**: Does the company manage debt responsibly?

   Platforms like Yahoo Finance, Morningstar, and Seeking Alpha provide easy access to this data.

2. **Understand the Company's Industry**
   Research the industry trends and challenges. A strong company in a growing sector often has more upside potential.

3. **Look at Valuation Metrics**
   - **P/E Ratio (Price-to-Earnings)**: Measures how much you're paying for $1 of the company's earnings.
   - **Dividend Yield**: Shows the annual dividend as a percentage of the stock price.

4. **Use Stock Screeners**
   Free tools like Finviz or Google Finance allow you to filter stocks based on specific criteria, such as market cap, dividend yield, or growth rate.

5. **Follow News and Analyst Reports**
   Staying informed about a company's latest developments can give you insights into potential opportunities or risks.

The stock market might seem complex at first, but with the right knowledge and tools, it becomes a powerful ally in your wealth-building journey. Whether you choose to invest in individual stocks, ETFs, or index funds, the key is to start with a clear understanding of your goals and risk tolerance.

In the next chapter, we'll explore another exciting wealth-building avenue: real estate. You'll learn how to get started in this time-tested investment strategy, even as a beginner.

Your journey into the stock market has begun. Keep learning, stay consistent, and watch your wealth grow!

Chapter 5
Real Estate Investing Made Simple

Real estate has long been one of the most reliable ways to build wealth. It's tangible, enduring, and offers multiple paths to generate income and grow your net worth. Whether it's owning rental properties, flipping houses, or investing in real estate funds, this asset class has something for everyone—no matter your budget or experience level.

But for many beginners, real estate investing seems out of reach. Perhaps you think you need a fortune to get started, or maybe the idea of managing tenants feels overwhelming. The truth is, there are plenty of entry points, even for those just starting their financial journey. This chapter will show you why real estate remains a cornerstone of wealth-building and how you can take your first steps toward owning a piece of it.

Why Real Estate is a Time-Tested Wealth-Building Tool

Real estate has been a wealth-building staple for centuries, and for good reason. It offers unique advantages that other investments simply can't match:

1. **Tangible Asset**: Unlike stocks or bonds, real estate is something you can see, touch, and use. It holds intrinsic value, no matter what happens in the economy.

2. **Multiple Streams of Income**: With real estate, you can earn money in several ways:
    - **Rental Income**: Monthly payments from tenants.
    - **Property Appreciation**: Over time, properties often increase in value.
    - **Tax Advantages**: Real estate offers deductions for expenses like mortgage interest, property taxes, and depreciation.

3. **Leverage**: Real estate allows you to use other people's money—usually through a mortgage—to purchase assets that grow in value. This means you can amplify your returns while only investing a fraction of the property's total cost.

4. **Inflation Hedge**: As the cost of living rises, so do property values and rents. This makes real estate a

powerful way to protect and grow your wealth over time.

Simply put, real estate creates opportunities to grow your money while providing stability in your investment portfolio.

Entry Points for Beginners

You don't need millions of dollars or a massive property portfolio to start investing in real estate. Here are some beginner-friendly ways to get started:

1. **REITs (Real Estate Investment Trusts)**
   If buying property seems overwhelming, REITs are a great way to invest in real estate without the hassle of owning physical assets.
   - REITs are companies that own, operate, or finance income-producing properties, such as office buildings, apartments, or shopping centers.
   - By purchasing shares in a REIT, you can earn a share of the income generated by these properties, often through dividends.
   - They're easy to buy and sell on the stock market, making them highly liquid.
2. **Fractional Real Estate Investing**
   New platforms like Fundrise or Roofstock make it

possible to buy small stakes in properties or real estate portfolios.

- These platforms pool money from multiple investors to purchase larger properties, such as apartment complexes or commercial buildings.
- You earn a portion of the rental income and appreciation, just like owning a slice of a bigger pie.

3. **House Hacking**

   This strategy involves purchasing a property and living in part of it while renting out the other units or rooms.

   - For example, you could buy a duplex, live in one unit, and rent out the other to cover your mortgage.
   - It's a fantastic way to build equity while keeping your living costs low.
   - House hacking is especially popular among young investors looking to start small and scale up.

These entry points allow you to dip your toes into real estate without taking on massive risks or responsibilities.

The Pros and Cons of Owning Rental Properties

Owning rental properties is one of the most popular forms of real estate investing. But like any investment, it comes with its own set of advantages and challenges.

Pros:

- **Steady Income**: Rental properties provide a consistent monthly cash flow.
- **Wealth Building**: Over time, tenants pay down your mortgage while your property appreciates.
- **Control**: Unlike stocks, where you're at the mercy of the market, you have direct control over your property's value through upgrades, management, and strategy.

Cons:

- **Time-Intensive**: Managing tenants, maintenance, and repairs can be demanding.
- **Upfront Costs**: Down payments, closing costs, and renovation expenses can add up.
- **Market Risk**: Real estate markets can fluctuate, affecting your property's value and rental demand.

While rental properties can be incredibly rewarding, it's important to understand the responsibilities involved and have a clear plan for managing them.

How to Evaluate a Real Estate Deal

Not all real estate deals are created equal. To ensure you're making a smart investment, consider these three key factors:

1. **Location**:
    - The old adage "location, location, location" holds true. A property's location determines its demand, rental income, and appreciation potential.
    - Look for areas with job growth, good schools, and access to amenities like public transportation and shopping.
2. **Cash Flow**:
    - Cash flow is the money left over after you've paid all expenses (mortgage, taxes, insurance, and maintenance). Positive cash flow ensures your property generates income rather than draining your resources.
3. **Appreciation Potential**:
    - While cash flow provides immediate income, appreciation grows your wealth over time.
    - Research market trends and talk to local real estate agents to gauge a property's long-term value potential.

Pro tip: Use tools like the **1% Rule** as a quick way to evaluate deals. This rule suggests that a property should generate at least 1% of its purchase price in monthly rental income. For example, a $200,000 property should bring in at least $2,000 per month in rent.

Real estate investing doesn't have to be complicated or intimidating. With the right approach, you can start small, learn the ropes, and gradually scale your investments. Whether you choose REITs, house hacking, or rental properties, real estate can provide the stability, income, and growth you need to achieve financial freedom.

In the next chapter, we'll explore other exciting ways to generate passive income—because building wealth is all about creating multiple streams of income. Let's keep moving forward!

Chapter 6
Other Passive Income Streams to Explore

Building wealth is like constructing a fortress—each income stream is a sturdy pillar that strengthens your financial foundation. While real estate and the stock market are excellent wealth-building tools, they're just two of many ways to generate passive income. Diversifying your income sources is not only smart; it's essential for long-term financial security. In this chapter, we'll explore additional passive income streams that can help you earn while you sleep, giving you more freedom and flexibility in your financial journey.

Bonds and Treasury Bills: Low-Risk, Steady-Return Investments

If you're looking for safe, reliable ways to grow your money, bonds and treasury bills (T-bills) are excellent options. These investments are often referred to as "fixed-income securities" because they provide regular, predictable returns.

How They Work:

- **Bonds** are essentially loans you give to a company, municipality, or government. In return, you earn interest over a specified period, and the borrower repays your principal at maturity.
- **Treasury Bills** are short-term loans to the government, often maturing in a year or less. They're considered one of the safest investments because they're backed by the full faith and credit of the government.

Why Consider Them?

- Low risk: These investments are far less volatile than stocks.
- Predictable income: You know exactly how much you'll earn over time.
- Portfolio balance: Bonds are a great way to offset riskier investments like stocks.

Pro tip: Consider investing in **bond ETFs** or **mutual funds** for easy diversification across multiple bonds.

Peer-to-Peer Lending: Pros, Cons, and Platforms to Start

Peer-to-peer (P2P) lending is an innovative way to earn passive income by lending money directly to individuals or small businesses through online platforms like LendingClub or Prosper.

How It Works:

- You act as the lender, providing funds for loans requested by borrowers.
- In return, you earn interest payments over time.

Pros:

- Higher potential returns than traditional savings or bonds.
- You can diversify your loans across multiple borrowers to reduce risk.

Cons:

- Risk of default: If a borrower fails to repay, you could lose your money.
- Not guaranteed: Unlike bank deposits, P2P lending isn't insured.

P2P lending works best as part of a diversified investment strategy. Start small, research each platform's track record, and spread your funds across multiple loans to minimize risk.

Dividend Investing: Creating a Consistent Income Stream

Imagine getting paid just for owning shares in a company—that's the beauty of dividend investing. Many companies reward their shareholders by distributing a portion of their profits as dividends.

Why Dividends Matter:

- **Steady Income**: Dividends provide a consistent cash flow, whether the stock market is up or down.
- **Compounding Power**: Reinvesting dividends allows you to buy more shares, accelerating your wealth-building.
- **Stability**: Dividend-paying companies are often established, financially stable businesses.

How to Get Started:

1. Look for **dividend aristocrats**—companies with a history of increasing dividends year after year.
2. Use platforms like Robinhood, M1 Finance, or Fidelity to invest in dividend-focused ETFs or individual stocks.
3. Reinvest your dividends automatically to maximize growth.

Dividend investing is a straightforward way to build a passive income stream that grows alongside your portfolio. Over time, these payouts can become a powerful source of financial freedom.

Digital and Intellectual Property: Royalties, Online Courses, and E-Books

The digital age has opened up exciting new opportunities to generate passive income. With a little creativity and effort upfront, you can create digital assets that pay you for years to come.

1. Royalties from Creative Works

If you're a musician, writer, or artist, royalties can provide a consistent income stream.

- **Music royalties**: Earn money every time your song is streamed, played, or licensed.
- **Book royalties**: Self-publish e-books or audiobooks on platforms like Amazon Kindle Direct Publishing or Audible.

2. Online Courses

If you have expertise in a particular subject, consider creating an online course.

- Platforms like Udemy, Teachable, and Skillshare allow you to share your knowledge and earn income every time someone enrolls.
- Courses on topics like coding, photography, or personal development are in high demand.

3. E-Books

Writing an e-book is another excellent way to monetize your expertise.

- Choose a niche topic with a dedicated audience, such as personal finance, fitness, or productivity.
- Once published, e-books require little maintenance and can generate income for years.

Why Digital Assets Work:

- Minimal overhead: Digital products have low production and distribution costs.
- Unlimited scalability: You can sell the same product to an unlimited number of people.
- Long-term income: A well-crafted digital asset can continue to sell long after you've created it.

Passive income streams like these are not only practical—they're empowering. They allow you to leverage your time, skills, and money to create wealth beyond your day job. By diversifying your sources of income, you're building a financial safety net that will support you through life's ups and downs.

In the next chapter, we'll dive into how to navigate risk as an investor and develop the confidence to keep building your financial future, no matter what challenges arise. Let's keep the momentum going!

Chapter 7
Navigating Risk and Building Confidence as an Investor

Investing can feel like stepping into the unknown—markets rise and fall, news headlines scream doom, and it's easy to second-guess your decisions. But here's the truth: risk is not the enemy; it's part of the process. The key to successful investing is learning how to manage risk while building the confidence to stay the course. In this chapter, we'll explore strategies to help you navigate market fluctuations, diversify your investments, and maintain a long-term perspective. Let's turn your fears into fuel for financial growth.

Understanding Market Fluctuations: Why Downturns Are Normal and Temporary

Imagine a rollercoaster. There are thrilling highs, nerve-wracking drops, and twists you didn't see coming—but the ride always comes back to the station. The stock market works the same way. Volatility is normal, and downturns are an inevitable part of the journey.

Why Downturns Happen:

- **Economic cycles**: Recessions and expansions are natural phases of the economy.
- **Market corrections**: Short-term drops (often 10-20%) occur as markets adjust to new information or overvaluations.
- **Global events**: Wars, pandemics, or political unrest can cause temporary uncertainty.

The Bigger Picture: Historically, markets recover and grow over time. The S&P 500, for example, has weathered crashes, recessions, and crises but consistently trended upward over decades.

Pro tip: When the market dips, think of it as a sale on investments. Downturns are opportunities to buy quality assets at lower prices.

How Diversification Protects Your Portfolio

Imagine betting your entire fortune on a single horse. If it wins, great—but if it stumbles, you lose everything. That's the risk of putting all your money into one investment. Diversification spreads your risk across different assets, reducing the impact of any single investment's performance.

How to Diversify:

1. **Invest in multiple asset classes**: Balance stocks, bonds, real estate, and cash equivalents.
2. **Spread across industries**: Don't put all your stock investments into one sector (e.g., tech or healthcare).
3. **Geographic diversity**: Invest in both domestic and international markets to mitigate regional risks.
4. **Use ETFs and index funds**: These are excellent tools for instant diversification, giving you exposure to hundreds of assets in one investment.

Diversification is like having a safety net. When one part of your portfolio underperforms, others can help cushion the blow, keeping you on track toward your financial goals.

The Importance of a Long-Term Perspective: "Time in the Market Beats Timing the Market"

The secret sauce of successful investing is patience. While the market's short-term movements may seem unpredictable, its long-term trajectory is remarkably consistent: upward.

Why Time Matters:

- **Compound growth accelerates**: The longer your money stays invested, the more it can grow exponentially.
- **Short-term noise fades**: Daily market fluctuations have little impact on a 20- or 30-year investment horizon.

The Myth of Market Timing:

Trying to predict when to buy or sell is a losing game. Even seasoned professionals struggle to consistently time the market. Missing just a few of the best-performing days can drastically reduce your returns.

Pro tip: Commit to "time in the market" by setting up automated, regular contributions. This ensures you're always investing, regardless of market conditions.

Overcoming the Fear of Losing Money: Practical Tips to Manage Emotions

Fear is one of the biggest barriers to building wealth. It can paralyze you into inaction or drive you to make impulsive decisions. But here's the good news: fear can be managed, and confidence can be built with the right mindset and strategies.

1. Educate Yourself

Knowledge is power. The more you understand how markets work, the less intimidating they become. Read books, follow reputable financial blogs, and surround yourself with informed voices.

2. Focus on Your Goals

When fear creeps in, remind yourself why you're investing: financial freedom, a secure retirement, or a better future for your family. Keeping your goals in mind can help you weather short-term turbulence.

3. Build a Safety Net

An emergency fund and a diversified portfolio act as psychological anchors, giving you peace of mind during market downturns.

4. Limit Emotional Reactions

- Avoid checking your portfolio daily—it amplifies stress.
- Set "rules" for yourself, like waiting 24 hours before making any major investment decisions.
- Stay disciplined by sticking to your financial plan, even when emotions run high.

5. Celebrate Progress

Track your wins, no matter how small. Seeing your investments grow over time, even modestly, reinforces positive behavior and builds your confidence.

Risk and fear are natural parts of investing, but they don't have to control you. With a long-term perspective, a diversified portfolio, and a steady hand during market fluctuations, you'll find that the rewards far outweigh the risks. Remember, every successful investor started as a beginner who learned to navigate uncertainty.

In the next chapter, we'll focus on building your investment portfolio—turning theory into action with practical steps and strategies for creating a balanced, thriving financial future. You've got this!

Chapter 8
Building Your Investment Portfolio

Now that you've built a strong financial foundation and gained confidence in navigating risks, it's time to assemble the engine of your wealth-building journey: your investment portfolio. Think of your portfolio as a carefully designed toolkit, built to work for your unique goals, risk tolerance, and timeline. In this chapter, we'll show you how to balance your investments, provide sample portfolios to fit various needs, and give you tools to easily manage and optimize your financial future.

Asset Allocation for Beginners: Balancing Stocks, Bonds, and Other Assets

Asset allocation is the cornerstone of successful investing. It's the art of dividing your money among different types of investments to strike the right balance between risk and reward.

Why Asset Allocation Matters

- **Risk management**: Different asset types respond differently to market conditions. When stocks dip, bonds or real estate may hold steady.
- **Customization**: Your allocation reflects your personal financial goals, risk tolerance, and investment timeline.
- **Growth and stability**: A balanced portfolio ensures you can grow wealth while minimizing the chance of severe losses.

Basic Asset Classes

1. **Stocks**: High-risk, high-reward investments that provide growth over time.
2. **Bonds**: Low-risk investments that offer steady, predictable returns.
3. **Real Estate**: A tangible asset that generates income and appreciates over time.
4. **Cash Equivalents**: Savings accounts, money market funds, or CDs for short-term needs and stability.

Rule of Thumb for Beginners

The percentage of stocks vs. bonds in your portfolio often depends on your age. A common guideline: Subtract your age from 100, and that's the percentage to invest in stocks. For example, if you're 30, consider 70% stocks and 30% bonds.

Pro tip: Don't forget to factor in other goals. If you're investing for retirement decades away, lean more heavily toward growth-oriented assets like stocks.

Sample Portfolio Setups for Different Goals and Risk Levels

1. Conservative Portfolio (Low Risk)

- 20% Stocks (e.g., blue-chip or dividend-paying stocks)
- 60% Bonds (e.g., government or high-quality corporate bonds)
- 10% Real Estate (e.g., REITs)
- 10% Cash or cash equivalents

Ideal for: Those nearing retirement or with a low risk tolerance.

2. Balanced Portfolio (Moderate Risk)

- 50% Stocks (a mix of growth and dividend-paying stocks)
- 30% Bonds
- 15% Real Estate
- 5% Cash

Ideal for: Mid-career professionals seeking steady growth with some protection.

3. Aggressive Portfolio (High Risk)

- 80% Stocks (growth and international stocks)
- 10% Real Estate
- 10% Bonds

Ideal for: Younger investors or those with a long investment horizon and high risk tolerance.

Pro tip: These are starting points. Customize your portfolio based on your preferences and goals.

How to Rebalance Your Portfolio: When and Why to Adjust Your Investments

Over time, your portfolio can drift from its original allocation. For example, if stocks perform well, they may take up a larger percentage of your portfolio than you intended, increasing your overall risk. Rebalancing restores your portfolio to its original balance.

When to Rebalance

- **Annually or semi-annually**: Set a regular schedule to review and adjust your portfolio.
- **When allocations shift significantly**: For example, if your stock allocation grows from 70%

to 80%, it might be time to sell some stocks and buy more bonds or other assets.

How to Rebalance

1. **Review your target allocation**: Compare it to your current portfolio.
2. **Sell overperforming assets**: Use the profits to buy underperforming ones.
3. **Automate with contributions**: Instead of selling, direct new investments into the underweighted assets to restore balance.

Pro tip: Use tax-advantaged accounts, like IRAs or 401(k)s, to rebalance without triggering taxable events.

Tools and Apps to Simplify Portfolio Management

Managing your portfolio doesn't have to be overwhelming. Modern technology offers a range of tools to help you track, analyze, and optimize your investments with ease.

1. Robo-Advisors

These automated platforms manage your portfolio for you based on your goals and risk tolerance. Examples include Betterment, Wealthfront, and Vanguard Digital Advisor.

2. Portfolio Trackers

Apps like Personal Capital, Mint, or Morningstar help you monitor your portfolio's performance and allocation in real time.

3. Brokerages with Built-in Tools

Platforms like Fidelity, Charles Schwab, and Robinhood offer tools for analysis, performance tracking, and rebalancing.

4. Educational Resources

Stay informed with apps like Investopedia or Yahoo Finance, which provide market updates, tutorials, and expert advice.

Building an investment portfolio is not a one-time task—it's a dynamic process that evolves with your life and goals. By mastering asset allocation, maintaining balance, and leveraging modern tools, you can create a portfolio that works for you, not against you.

In the next chapter, we'll dive into the often-overlooked topic of taxes—how they impact your investments and strategies to keep more of your hard-earned money working toward your financial freedom. Stay inspired, and keep moving forward!

Chapter 9
Tax Basics Every Investor Should Know

Taxes are a fact of life, but for investors, understanding how taxes work can make the difference between growing your wealth efficiently and watching a chunk of it disappear. The good news? With the right strategies, you can minimize your tax burden and keep more of your hard-earned money working for you. This chapter will empower you to navigate the tax landscape with confidence, ensuring your investments are as tax-efficient as possible.

Tax-Advantaged Accounts: 401(k)s, IRAs, HSAs, and More

Tax-advantaged accounts are one of the most powerful tools available to investors. They allow you to either defer taxes or grow your money tax-free, depending on the type of account.

1. 401(k) Plans

- **What they are**: Employer-sponsored retirement accounts with pre-tax or Roth (after-tax) contribution options.
- **Benefits**: Contributions to traditional 401(k)s reduce your taxable income now, and investments grow tax-deferred until withdrawal. Roth 401(k)s grow tax-free, and withdrawals are tax-free in retirement.
- **Employer match**: Many employers match contributions, effectively giving you free money.

2. IRAs (Individual Retirement Accounts)

- **Traditional IRA**: Contributions may be tax-deductible, and earnings grow tax-deferred. Withdrawals are taxed as income.
- **Roth IRA**: Contributions are made with after-tax dollars, but investments grow and can be withdrawn tax-free in retirement.
- **Contribution limits**: As of 2024, you can contribute up to $6,500 annually ($7,500 if age 50 or older).

3. HSAs (Health Savings Accounts)

- **What they are**: Accounts tied to high-deductible health insurance plans.

- **Triple tax advantage**: Contributions are tax-deductible, growth is tax-free, and withdrawals for qualified medical expenses are tax-free.
- **Pro tip**: Use HSAs as a stealth retirement account by letting the funds grow for future medical costs.

4. Education Accounts

- **529 Plans**: Tax-advantaged accounts for educational expenses. Contributions grow tax-free, and withdrawals for qualified education expenses are not taxed.

By maximizing contributions to these accounts, you're not only saving for the future but also reducing your taxable income today.

How Dividends, Capital Gains, and Losses Are Taxed

As an investor, understanding how your earnings are taxed helps you make smarter decisions.

1. Dividends

- **Qualified dividends**: Taxed at lower capital gains rates (0%, 15%, or 20%, depending on your income).
- **Non-qualified dividends**: Taxed at your regular income tax rate.

2. Capital Gains

- **Short-term capital gains**: Earned on investments held for less than a year and taxed at your ordinary income rate.
- **Long-term capital gains**: Earned on investments held for more than a year and taxed at lower rates (0%, 15%, or 20%).
- **Pro tip**: Holding investments longer can significantly reduce your tax liability.

3. Capital Losses

- If an investment loses value, you can use those losses to offset gains, reducing your taxable income.
- You can also deduct up to $3,000 of losses against your regular income annually and carry forward unused losses to future years.

Strategies to Minimize Your Tax Liability as an Investor

Tax efficiency is about keeping more of what you earn. Here are strategies to help you minimize your tax burden:

1. Use Tax-Advantaged Accounts

Maximize contributions to accounts like 401(k)s, IRAs, and HSAs. These accounts shield your earnings from taxes, either now or in the future.

2. Hold Investments Long-Term

Aim for long-term capital gains rates by holding onto investments for more than a year.

3. Invest in Tax-Efficient Funds

- Index funds and ETFs generally produce fewer taxable events than actively managed funds.
- Look for funds labeled "tax-efficient" or "tax-managed."

4. Harvest Losses

Sell underperforming investments to realize losses, which can offset gains or reduce your taxable income.

5. Focus on Tax-Free Income

- Invest in municipal bonds, which often generate tax-free income at the federal and state level.
- Consider Roth IRAs for tax-free growth and withdrawals.

6. Pay Attention to Asset Location

- Place high-growth investments in tax-advantaged accounts to defer taxes.
- Hold tax-efficient investments (e.g., municipal bonds) in taxable accounts.

When to Consult a Tax Professional

While you can handle many tax strategies on your own, there are times when consulting a tax professional can save you money and headaches:

- **Complex investments**: If you're investing in real estate, foreign markets, or private equity, professional advice is invaluable.
- **High income**: Tax professionals can help you find advanced strategies to reduce your liability.
- **Changing laws**: Tax laws evolve, and an expert can keep you compliant while optimizing your returns.

Investing in a tax professional is like investing in your portfolio—it's a smart way to protect and grow your wealth.

Taxes might not be the most exciting part of investing, but mastering them is essential for long-term success. By leveraging tax-advantaged accounts, understanding how your earnings are taxed, and applying strategic tax-saving methods, you can supercharge your wealth-building journey.

In the next chapter, we'll talk about consistency and discipline—the secret ingredients that turn good intentions into lifelong financial freedom. Stay focused, stay inspired, and keep building your future!

Chapter 10

Staying the Course and Growing Your Wealth

Investing is not a sprint; it's a marathon. The most successful investors aren't those who made a quick fortune but those who stayed consistent, avoided unnecessary risks, and allowed time to work its magic. Building wealth is as much about mindset as it is about strategy. In this chapter, we'll dive into the habits, tools, and perspectives you need to stay on track and keep growing your wealth, no matter what life or the markets throw your way.

The Power of Consistency: How Small, Regular Investments Lead to Massive Growth

When it comes to wealth building, consistency beats perfection every time. Many people make the mistake of waiting for the "perfect" moment to invest or trying to save up a large sum before they begin. But the truth is, even small, regular investments can snowball into significant wealth over time.

1. The Magic of Compound Growth

Every dollar you invest isn't just money—it's a worker that generates more money for you. Over time, your earnings start earning their own earnings, creating an exponential growth curve. This is the power of compounding.

- For example, investing just $200 a month at an 8% annual return could grow to over $600,000 in 40 years.
- The earlier you start, the more powerful this effect becomes.

2. The Habit of Automation

Consistency becomes effortless when you automate your investments. Set up automatic transfers to your investment accounts each month, treating them like non-negotiable bills. This "set it and forget it" approach keeps your plan on track regardless of market conditions or personal distractions.

3. Focus on Progress, Not Perfection

It's better to invest small amounts regularly than to wait for a "perfect" opportunity or save for a massive initial investment. Small steps add up to big results.

Avoiding Common Pitfalls: Emotional Decisions, Chasing Trends, and Overleveraging

Even the most disciplined investors face temptations that can derail their plans. Staying the course means recognizing these pitfalls and actively avoiding them.

1. Emotional Decisions

- **Market fluctuations**: When the market dips, it's natural to feel fear. But selling in a panic locks in losses that would otherwise recover over time.
- **FOMO (Fear of Missing Out)**: Jumping on "hot" investments out of fear of being left behind often leads to costly mistakes.

Solution: Stick to your plan. Remember, markets are cyclical, and downturns are normal. Stay focused on the long-term.

2. Chasing Trends

Every year, there's a new buzzworthy investment—cryptocurrencies, meme stocks, or speculative tech startups. While some trends may deliver short-term gains, they often come with significant risk.

- Ask yourself: "Does this fit my long-term goals and risk tolerance?"

3. Overleveraging

Using borrowed money (leverage) to invest can amplify returns, but it also magnifies losses. If the market turns against you, it could wipe out your portfolio and leave you in debt.

Solution: Stick to what you can afford. Build wealth sustainably without taking on unnecessary risk.

Tracking Your Progress and Celebrating Milestones

Investing is a journey, and every step forward deserves recognition. Tracking your progress helps you stay motivated and make informed adjustments along the way.

1. Use Tools to Monitor Your Portfolio

- **Apps and software**: Platforms like Personal Capital, Mint, or your brokerage's dashboard can give you a clear picture of your portfolio's performance.
- **Key metrics**: Track your net worth, investment returns, and progress toward specific financial goals.

2. Review and Adjust Regularly

- **Quarterly reviews**: Assess your portfolio's performance every three months. Are you on track to meet your goals?

- **Rebalancing**: If one asset class has grown disproportionately, rebalance to maintain your desired asset allocation.

3. Celebrate Small Wins

Every milestone—whether it's your first $1,000 invested, your first dividend payment, or hitting a major savings goal—is worth celebrating. Recognizing your progress keeps you motivated and reinforces positive habits.

The Importance of Continuing Education: Staying Informed as Markets Evolve

The world of investing is always changing. New technologies, industries, and opportunities emerge every year. To grow your wealth consistently, commit to being a lifelong learner.

1. Stay Curious

- Follow credible financial news sources like CNBC, Bloomberg, or Morningstar.
- Listen to podcasts, read books, or join online communities focused on personal finance and investing.

2. Learn from Experience

Every investment, whether successful or not, teaches valuable lessons. Reflect on your past decisions to improve your strategy moving forward.

3. Seek Guidance When Needed

As your portfolio grows, consider working with a financial advisor to optimize your investments. Look for someone who aligns with your goals and values.

Staying the course is about more than discipline—it's about believing in your long-term vision. Remember, building wealth is a marathon, not a sprint. By staying consistent, avoiding pitfalls, tracking your progress, and continuing to learn, you're setting yourself up for a lifetime of financial freedom.

In the next chapter, we'll bring everything together with a step-by-step guide to making your first investment. You're almost there—stay inspired, and let's take that final leap together!

Chapter 11
A Step-by-Step Guide to Your First Investment

Congratulations! You've come a long way. By now, you've built a solid financial foundation, learned the basics of investing, and started crafting a strategy tailored to your goals. The next step? Taking action. In this chapter, we'll walk you through the practical steps to make your first investment. No jargon, no overwhelm —just clear, actionable guidance to help you take that exciting leap into the world of investing.

How to Open a Brokerage Account

The first step in your investment journey is opening a brokerage account. Think of a brokerage account as your gateway to the stock market and other investment opportunities.

1. Choose the Right Brokerage

Look for a platform that suits your needs as a beginner. Consider the following:

- **User-friendly interface**: Platforms like Fidelity, Charles Schwab, or Robinhood are designed with simplicity in mind.
- **Low or no fees**: Many brokerages now offer commission-free trading.
- **Investment options**: Ensure the brokerage offers the stocks, ETFs, or mutual funds you're interested in.
- **Educational resources**: Some platforms provide tutorials, articles, and tools to help you learn as you invest.

2. Gather Your Information

To open an account, you'll need:

- Your Social Security Number (or equivalent identification number in your country).
- A valid ID (driver's license, passport, etc.).
- Bank account details for transferring funds.

3. Complete the Application

Most brokerages allow you to open an account online in just a few minutes. You'll answer questions about your income, financial goals, and risk tolerance. Be honest—

this helps the platform provide tailored recommendations.

4. Fund Your Account

Transfer money from your bank to your brokerage account. Start with an amount you're comfortable with—remember, even small investments can grow significantly over time.

Step-by-Step Guide to Buying Your First Stock, ETF, or Fund

With your brokerage account funded, it's time to make your first investment. Let's break it down step by step:

1. Decide What to Buy

- **Stocks**: If you want to own a piece of a specific company, start with a blue-chip stock or one from an industry you understand.
- **ETFs (Exchange-Traded Funds)**: These are beginner-friendly because they offer instant diversification. Look for ETFs that track major indices like the S&P 500.
- **Mutual Funds**: Ideal for long-term investors who prefer professional management.

2. Research Your Investment

Before you buy, take a few minutes to review:

- The company or fund's history and performance.
- Analyst opinions (most brokerages provide free insights).
- Any fees associated with the investment.

3. Place Your Order

- Log in to your brokerage account.
- Search for the stock, ETF, or fund you want to buy using its name or ticker symbol (e.g., AAPL for Apple or SPY for an S&P 500 ETF).
- Choose the type of order:
    - **Market order**: Buys immediately at the current price.
    - **Limit order**: Sets a specific price at which you're willing to buy.
- Enter the number of shares or dollar amount you want to invest.
- Review the details and click "Buy."

Congratulations—you've just made your first investment!

Setting Up Automated Contributions for Hands-Off Growth

Investing doesn't have to be time-consuming. Automation makes it easy to stay consistent without constantly monitoring the market.

1. Schedule Automatic Transfers

Most brokerages let you set up recurring transfers from your bank account. Decide on an amount and frequency (e.g., $100 every payday) that aligns with your budget.

2. Enable Automatic Investing

Some platforms offer automated investment plans, where your contributions are automatically allocated to your chosen stocks, ETFs, or funds. This strategy is particularly effective for dollar-cost averaging, ensuring you invest consistently regardless of market fluctuations.

3. Revisit Periodically

While automation handles the heavy lifting, check in every few months to ensure your contributions align with your financial goals and adjust as needed.

Checklist to Review Before Making Your First Investment Decision

Before clicking "Buy," use this checklist to confirm you're ready:

- **Emergency Fund**: Do you have 3–6 months of living expenses saved?
- **Debt Check**: Have you addressed high-interest debt that could eat into your returns?

- **Risk Tolerance**: Are you comfortable with the level of risk involved in your chosen investment?
- **Financial Goals**: Does this investment align with your short-, mid-, or long-term objectives?
- **Research Done**: Have you reviewed the investment's performance, fees, and growth potential?
- **Diversification**: Does this investment contribute to a balanced portfolio?
- **Funds Available**: Are you using money you can afford to invest (not needed for immediate expenses)?

If you've checked all these boxes, you're ready to invest with confidence!

Your first investment is more than a financial transaction—it's a declaration of your commitment to building a brighter future. It's the moment you take control of your financial destiny and start putting your money to work for you.

Remember, every great investor started where you are now: with a first step, a first dollar, and a vision for something bigger. Celebrate this milestone—it's the beginning of an incredible journey.

In the next chapter, we'll recap your journey and remind you why investing is for everyone. You've got this—your path to financial freedom is well underway!

Conclusion
Investing is for Everyone

You made it to the end of this book, and what a journey it's been! Along the way, you've learned that investing isn't just for Wall Street tycoons or financial experts—it's for everyone, including you. Whether you're starting with $5 or $50,000, the principles remain the same: consistency, patience, and a commitment to growth can transform your financial future.

From Beginner to Confident Investor

We began by breaking down the myths that hold so many people back from investing. You've built a solid foundation by getting your finances in order, explored different types of investments, and gained a clear understanding of how to manage risk and build a portfolio. Step by step, you've acquired the tools and knowledge needed to make informed decisions.

You've learned that:

- **Investing is about growth.** Your money has the potential to work harder than you ever could.
- **Risk is manageable.** With diversification, research, and a long-term perspective, you can face market fluctuations with confidence.
- **Small steps lead to big results.** Starting small isn't a disadvantage—it's how most successful investors began.

Now, the only thing left to do is take that first step.

Start Small, Start Today

The hardest part of any journey is taking the first step. It's easy to get caught up in "what ifs" or feel overwhelmed by the wealth of information out there. But here's the truth: no one feels 100% ready when they start. The key is to start anyway.

Remember, it's not about perfection—it's about progress. Each dollar you invest, each lesson you learn, and each mistake you make will bring you closer to your financial goals. Even the smallest action today can lead to life-changing results tomorrow.

The Power of Patience and Discipline

Investing is a marathon, not a sprint. There will be ups and downs, moments of doubt, and times when you're tempted to give up. But wealth is built through patience, discipline, and a commitment to the long game.

Think about this:

- Every market correction is an opportunity, not a setback.
- Every small contribution is a brick in the foundation of your financial freedom.
- Every year you stay consistent brings you closer to your dreams.

The sooner you start, the more time your investments have to grow. Let compound interest work its magic and watch as your financial future transforms.

Final Call to Action: Take Control of Your Future

Now is the time to act. You have the knowledge, the tools, and the confidence to make investing a part of your life. Don't wait for the "perfect" moment—it doesn't exist. The best day to start investing was yesterday; the next best day is today.

Imagine where you could be a year from now, five years from now, or even decades down the road. Picture the financial freedom you'll create—not just for yourself, but for your loved ones and future generations.

This isn't the end of your journey; it's the beginning of something extraordinary. Take a deep breath, open that brokerage account, and make your first investment. Trust in the process, believe in your ability to succeed, and stay the course.

You've got this. Your future is bright, your potential is limitless, and your financial freedom is within reach. Now, go out there and make it happen.

"The best way to predict the future is to create it."

Go create your future—starting today.

Investment Checklist: Key Questions to Ask Before Making Any Investment

Making informed investment decisions is crucial to building a successful portfolio. Use this checklist to evaluate potential investments and ensure they align with your financial goals and risk tolerance.

1. Does this investment align with my financial goals?

- Is this investment for short-term, mid-term, or long-term goals?
- Will it help me reach specific milestones like buying a house, funding education, or retiring comfortably?

2. Do I understand how this investment works?

- What is the asset type (e.g., stock, bond, real estate, ETF, etc.)?

- How does it generate returns (e.g., appreciation, dividends, interest)?
- Are there any special conditions, like lock-in periods or penalties for early withdrawal?

3. What are the risks involved?

- What are the potential downsides of this investment?
- How much of my principal could I lose?
- Is the investment highly volatile, or does it have a history of steady returns?

4. What is the potential reward?

- What is the historical or expected rate of return?
- Does the potential return justify the risks I'm taking?
- Are there other investments with similar returns but lower risks?

5. Does it fit my risk tolerance?

- Am I comfortable with the level of uncertainty associated with this investment?
- Will I lose sleep if the value fluctuates or drops temporarily?

6. Is this investment diversified?

- Does it complement or overlap with my existing investments?
- Does it help balance my portfolio by adding exposure to different sectors, asset classes, or regions?

7. What are the costs and fees?

- Are there upfront costs, management fees, or transaction fees?
- How do these costs impact my overall returns?
- Are there more cost-effective alternatives available?

8. What is the time horizon?

- How long do I plan to hold this investment?
- Is it suitable for my time horizon (e.g., short-term, medium-term, or long-term)?

9. What are the tax implications?

- Will I owe taxes on dividends, interest, or capital gains?

- Can I hold this investment in a tax-advantaged account like a 401(k) or IRA?
- Are there strategies I can use to minimize my tax liability?

10. How liquid is this investment?

- How quickly can I sell or access my money if needed?
- Are there penalties or fees for early withdrawal or selling?

11. Have I done my due diligence?

- Have I researched the company, fund, or asset thoroughly?
- Do I understand the market or industry trends impacting this investment?
- Have I read credible reviews or sought advice from trusted experts?

12. Am I prepared for the worst-case scenario?

- If this investment loses value, how will it impact my overall financial health?
- Do I have a diversified portfolio to cushion potential losses?

- Can I afford to hold the investment through market downturns?

Before You Invest

Before making any investment, ask yourself:

- **Why am I investing in this?**
- **What do I expect to gain?**
- **What's the worst that could happen, and can I handle it?**

When in doubt, seek advice from a financial advisor or trusted mentor. A thoughtful approach to investing is the key to building lasting wealth.

Use this checklist as your guide, and you'll move forward with confidence in every investment decision you make!

www.ingramcontent.com/pod-product-compliance
Lightning Source LLC
Chambersburg PA
CBHW070354230526
45471CB00006B/2559